THE NEW ANDY CAPP COLLECTION
NUMBER 2

THE NEW ANDY CAPP COLLECTION

NUMBER 2

D&C

David and Charles

Edited by Duncan Ion

Cartoons: Roger Kettle & Roger Mahoney
Graphics: Richard Sunderland

Visit Andy at www.andycapp.com

A DAVID & CHARLES BOOK
David & Charles is a subsidiary of F+W (UK) Ltd.,
an F+W Publications Inc. company

First published in the UK in 2005

A catalogue record for this book is available from the British Library.

ISBN 0 7153 2165 X

Printed in Singapore by KHL Printing Co Pte Ltd.
for David & Charles
Brunel House   Newton Abbot   Devon

Visit our website at **www.davidandcharles.co.uk**

David & Charles books are available from all good bookshops;
alternatively you can contact our Orderline on 0870 9908222 or
write to us at FREEPOST EX2 110, D&C Direct, Newton Abbot,
TQ12 4ZZ (no stamp required UK mainland).

THE MAN WHO GOT DOWN ON ONE KNEE AND PROPOSED TO ME

IF HE HAD TO DO IT TODAY, HE'D PROBABLY GET UP ON ONE ELBOW

THANKS, ANDY!

THAT'S ALL RIGHT, VICAR — ENJOYED IT!

PITY HE DOESN'T BELONG TO MY DENOMINATION — WE COULD DO WITH A BIT MORE BITE IN OUR CHURCH FOOTBALL TEAM —

NO PROBLEM. I'LL HAVE A WORD WITH HIM. WHEN IT COMES TO BEING OFFERED A GAME OF FOOTBALL HE'S AN ANYTHINGARIAN

COULD YOU HELP US OUT, ANDY? WE NEED A REFEREE FOR OUR CLUB SNOOKER TOURNAMENT THIS EVENING

SURE, DAVE—

MIND YOU, I PROMISED TO TAKE FLO OUT TONIGHT. NEVER MIND, I'LL TRY TO LET HER DOWN LIGHTLY...

LET HER DOWN LIGHTLY—?

WHAT CAN I SAY THAT I HAVEN'T ALREADY SAID TO HIM? ALL I WANT IS TO GET MESELF T' BED...

GRRRR

I'M TERRIBLY SORRY, PET—I SWEAR I'LL BE EARLIER IN THE FUTURE

DON'T KNOW WHY I WASTE MY TIME — A DIRTY LOOK IS AS GOOD AS A SPEECH ANY DAY

WELL?

I GOT SENT OFF FOR THROWING THE REF'S WHISTLE AWAY

THAT SEEMS A BIT HARSH

IT WAS STILL IN HIS MOUTH AT THE TIME

BILLY'S WEDDING WENT WELL, GIVEN THE CIRCUMSTANCES

APART FROM THE AWKWARD MOMENT WHEN HE WENT TO PUT THE RING ON THE BRIDE'S FINGER ....

.... AND THE GUARD HAD TO UNLOCK HIS HANDCUFFS

VERY DISCREET, THOUGH

SLIMMING CLUB

I'VE LOST EIGHT POUNDS!

I'VE PUT ON ONE

HOW DID YOU GET ON?

GREAT— RUBY AND I HAVE LOST SEVEN POUNDS BETWEEN US!

GOODNIGHT, SPORT

GOODNIGHT, DEAR—

GIVE THE LASS A BREAK! SHE'S PROBABLY GOING BACK TO SOME GLOOMY BED-SIT ROOM...

HEY, PET! WOULD YOU CARE FOR ANOTHER, THEN MEBBE A FISH AND CHIP SUPPER AT CLOSING TIME?

ARE YOU KIDDING? YOU'VE COST ME ENOUGH ALREADY!!

TCH! YOU GO OUT OF YOUR WAY TO BE SOCIABLE...

YOU'RE ASKING WHY I'M LATE?

YES

YOU MEAN ME — WHY I'M LATE?

YES

YOU MEAN LATE LIKE NOT ON TIME?

YES

YOU'RE DESPERATELY TRYING TO THINK UP AN EXCUSE, AREN'T YOU?

YOU MEAN AN EXCUSE FOR ME?

THE NEW PEOPLE ARE MOVING IN ACROSS THE STREET

THE MAN'S CARRYING A POOL CUE, A FISHING ROD AND TWELVE CANS OF BEER

AND THERE'S MY HUSBAND HUGGING HIM

TCH! WE REALLY NEED A NEW FRIDGE

GOOD IDEA, PET

WE COULD AFFORD A DEPOSIT ON ONE IF YOU CUT BACK ON BEER FOR A WHILE

THEY SAY SOUR MILK'S REALLY GOOD FOR YOU

THIS IS JUST AN INFORMAL MEETING, MISTER CAPP, TO DISCUSS YOUR FINANCES

BARKLOYDS BANK

WHERE ARE THEY?

BARKLOYDS BANK

THERE'S AN IDEA FOR THE SUMMER, CHALKIE

WE COULD GO DRINKING AT GOLF TOURNAMENTS

WHY ARE WOMEN SUCH NAGS?

IT'S IN THEIR BLOOD

LAST NIGHT, RUBY WENT ON AND ON AT ME — "TAKE YOUR SHOES OFF! PUT THEM BY THE DOOR!"

IN THE END, I GOT OUT OF BED AND TOOK THEM OFF JUST TO SHUT HER UP

IT'LL BE OUR ANNIVERSARY SOON, PET. WHAT DID WE DO LAST YEAR?

OH, I REMEMBER — A FEW DRINKS AND A CHINESE MEAL

MAYBE THIS YEAR, I CAN COME TOO

MUM WAS WONDERING IF YOU COULD FIX HER CUPBOARD DOOR FOR HER

WHEN WILL I SAY YOU'LL LET HER DOWN?

GREAT SERMON ON SUNDAY, VICAR — DAVID AND GOLIATH!

AH, YES — A POWERFUL ALLEGORY ON SEVERAL LEVELS, NOT LEAST THE STRUGGLE AGAINST SUPERIOR ODDS

I LIKED IT WHEN THE STONE BOPPED HIM!

SHE'S NICE!

IF I WAS TWENTY YEARS YOUNGER...

YOU'D BE THE SAME AGE AS HER DAD

YOU'RE NOT A GREAT ONE FOR EGO-BOOSTING, ARE YOU, CHALKIE?

I'M GOING TO HAVE TO GIVE THIS GAME UP

I WAS PANTING SO MUCH, I COULD HARDLY SWEAR AT THE REFEREE!

HOW ABOUT GOING OUT FOR A MEAL TOMORROW? WE HAVEN'T BEEN OUT FOR AGES

IT CAN'T BE *THAT* LONG

PUT IT THIS WAY ...

...THE LAST TIME WE WENT, CONFETTI KEPT FALLING OFF MY HAT INTO THE SOUP

ALL I WANTED HER TO DO WAS FETCH ME A BEER FROM THE FRIDGE

SURELY THAT'S NOT TOO MUCH TO ASK?

I GUESS NOT

BUT NO, NO — SHE STAYED ON THE ROOF REPAIRING THE TILES!

YIPPEE!

YOUR WEIGHT

WELL DONE, PET— YOU'VE OBVIOUSLY LOST A POUND OR TWO

I'VE PUT ON FOUR— BETTY BROWN WAS WATCHING FROM ACROSS THE STREET

YOU'RE BACK FROM THE PUB EARLY— WHAT HAPPENED?

A COMBINATION OF FOUR THINGS THAT SHOULDN'T BE ALLOWED

YOUR MUM, GIN, KARAOKE AND "HOW MUCH IS THAT DOGGIE IN THE WINDOW?"

I BUMPED INTO BILLY BLOGGS TODAY— REMEMBER HIM FROM SCHOOL?

OF COURSE!

ALWAYS IN TROUBLE— GOT THROWN OUT FOR DRINKING AND SETTING FIRE TO THE GYM

HELLUVA TEACHER, THOUGH

ONE OF THE BEST

SO YOU WERE DRINKING WITH FRED TILL CLOSING TIME?

YES

HE PHONED JUST AFTER YOU LEFT TO SAY HE COULDN'T MAKE IT TO THE PUB — *HE WASN'T THERE!*

I THOUGHT HE WAS QUIET

MARRIAGE GUIDANCE

THAT MIGHT BE CHALKIE — I GAVE HIM YOUR NUMBER SO HE COULD KEEP ME UP TO DATE WITH THE FOOTBALL SCORES

RING RING

IT'S REALLY WEIRD HAVING FLO'S MUM STAY WITH US FOR A COUPLE OF DAYS

SHE'S GOT THIS REALLY DEEP VOICE WHILE FLO'S IS QUITE HIGH

HAVE YOU EVER BEEN NAGGED IN HARMONY?

WHEN MOST PEOPLE COUNT TO TEN, THEY USE THE TIME TO CALM THEMSELVES DOWN

HE USES IT TO TAKE AIM

TCH! THE WAGES SOME OF THESE FOOTBALLERS GET— THREE MILLION A YEAR!

LET'S SEE — THAT WORKS OUT AT ABOUT ONE POINT FIVE MILLION A YEAR

HE CALCULATES SALARIES IN BEERS

FLO WON'T BE HOME FOR AGES — I'D BETTER GET MYSELF SOMETHING TO EAT

"EMPTY CONTENTS INTO A SAUCEPAN AND BRING TO A BOIL, STIRRING CONTINUOUSLY"

"STIRRING CONTINUOUSLY"?

FLO WILL BE HOME SOON

THOSE NEWLYWEDS ARE MOVING IN ACROSS THE STREET— I THINK YOU'LL LIKE HIM

SHE'S CARRYING HIM OVER THE THRESHOLD

SO YOU'VE JUST MOVED TO THE AREA?

THIS AFTERNOON

THOUGHT I'D GO FOR A BEER WHILE THE WIFE UNPACKED AND GOT MY DINNER READY

I THINK THAT'S WHAT'S CALLED "INSTANT BONDING"

IT'S 2 a.m.—YOU MUST HAVE WOKEN THE ENTIRE STREET

WOULD YOU LIKE TO EXPLAIN WHY YOU WERE SINGING "THE GREEN, GREEN GRASS OF HOME" AT THE TOP OF YOUR VOICE?

I DON'T KNOW THE WORDS TO "DELILAH"

PETER'S MOVED FROM BANKING TO ACCOUNTANCY

HE FELT IT WAS TIME FOR A CAREER CHANGE

ANDY DID THAT THIRTY YEARS AGO

HE MOVED FROM THE ARMCHAIR TO THE COUCH

SIGH

WHAT'S UP, VICAR?

CHURCH ATTENDANCE, ANDY— LAST NIGHT'S WAS THE LOWEST EVER

WHEN I SAID, "AMEN," IT ECHOED FOR TWENTY MINUTES

LOANS

NO, I'M AFRAID YOUR REPAYMENTS WOULD HAVE TO BE MADE IN CASH

LOANS

HAVING YOUR WIFE WASH OUR DISHES IS NOT AN OPTION

SIGH! FRIDAY NIGHT

A FEW YEARS BACK, WE'D HAVE BEEN OUT PAINTING THE TOWN RED

NOWADAYS, WE CAN'T EVEN MANAGE HALF THE UNDERCOAT

THANK GOODNESS YOU'RE BACK— THAT DRIPPING TAP IN THE KITCHEN'S BEEN DRIVING ME MAD

I WAS AT THE OPTICIAN'S TODAY — IT TURNS OUT I'M COLOR BLIND

IT CAME AS A BIG SHOCK TO ME — A BOLT FROM THE GREEN! HEH! HEH!

HOW LONG HAVE YOU BEEN WORKING ON THAT ONE?

AWHILE

YOU'RE LATE!

TRIP

THINK OF SOMETHING CLEVER —

HAS IT EVER OCCURED TO YOU THAT YOU MIGHT BE *EARLY*

WORST EVER EXCUSE?

PROBABLY

ALL THAT EXPENSE TO GO TO THE GAME AND WE LOSE 8-0!

LET'S DROWN OUR SORROWS

DROWN OUR SORROWS? WE'RE BROKE!

WE CAN'T EVEN HOLD OUR HEADS UNDERWATER FOR A SECOND!

...SO FLO OPENED THE INVITATION

HAVE YOU NOTICED HOW WOMEN NEVER SAY, "WE'VE BEEN INVITED TO A WEDDING"?

IT'S ALWAYS "WE'VE BEEN INVITED TO A WEDDING I'LL NEED A NEW HAT"— ALL IN ONE SENTENCE

SOMEONE SEEMS HAPPY—I PRESUME YOUR HORSE WON

THAT'S A BIT UNFAIR, VICAR—ASSUMING MY HAPPINESS IS LINKED TO THE EVILS OF GAMBLING

WHAT PRICE DID IT WIN AT?

TEN TO ONE

I'D LIKE TO TRY ON THIS DRESS, PLEASE

SIZE 12?

THIS IS A CHANGING ROOM—NOT A SECRET GATEWAY TO THE LAND OF MIRACLES

I'M LATE, I'M BROKE AND I'M COLD

IT'S STARTING TO RAIN AND I'VE FORGOTTEN MY KEY

DING DONG

I'M AT THE WRONG HOUSE AND THIS EVENING JUST KEEPS ON GETTING BETTER

CLAUSTROPHOBIA? NO, THAT'S NOT IT

AGORAPHOBIA? NO, THAT'S NOT IT EITHER

WHAT'S THE WORD FOR THE FEAR OF SPI—

JUST KILL IT!

CHALKIE'S BEEN TALKING ABOUT A SECOND HONEYMOON

YOU KNOW, GOING BACK TO THE SAME PLACE WE WENT FIRST TIME ROUND

THAT SOUNDS NICE

I'M NOT SURE I COULD SIT THROUGH UNITED VERSUS CITY AGAIN

THE USUAL, ANDY?

I SUPPOSE SO....

...ALTHOUGH I WAS THINKING ABOUT TRYING SOMETHING DIFFERENT FOR A CHANGE

YOU COULD PAY FOR IT

THIS CLONING BUSINESS IS AMAZING!

IMAGINE HAVING AN IDENTICAL REPLICA OF YOURSELF!

HE COULD BE ASLEEP ON THE COUCH AND DRINKING IN THE PUB AT THE SAME TIME

FANCY A DRINK IN THERE?

TOO UP-MARKET FOR US, CHALKIE

WINE BAR

THEY DON'T HAVE A DARTS TEAM — THEY HAVE A POLO TEAM

WINE BAR

WE WERE HOPING YOU AND ANDY COULD COME FOR A MEAL AT OUR HOUSE ON SATURDAY

IS THERE ANYTHING ANDY DOESN'T LIKE?

GOING FOR A MEAL AT SOMEONE'S HOUSE WHEN HE COULD BE IN THE PUB

NEW FACE, JACK, AND PRETTY WITH IT—

YOU'RE WASTING YOUR TIME, ANDY—SHE'S A SUNDAY SCHOOL TEACHER

OH, I DON'T KNOW, JACK—WITH LOOKS LIKE THAT, SHE CAN'T BE ALL GOOD

ARE YOU LISTENING? I SAID I'VE NEVER BEEN SO MISERABLE—

I'M LISTENING, BUT WHAT CAN I DO?

YOU COULD AT LEAST FEEL FOR ME!

NOT EVEN HALF A PINT, IF YOU DON'T BELIEVE ME, COME AND FEEL FOR YOURSELF

DID THE CARPENTER COME, PET?

YES, BUT HE WOULDN'T TACKLE THE JOB, SAID IT WAS NEXT TO IMPOSSIBLE

WHAT HAPPENS NOW?

YOU KNOW ME, PET, WHEN THEY SAY A THING CAN'T BE DONE

DEFINITELY—

DON'T BOTHER TO TRY

Printed in Great Britain
by Amazon

11122044R00074